The Rocking Chair Book

The Rocking Chair Book

A Spiritual Journey
From My Front Porch

Rena K.

*For Andy C., who heard this story first
and convinced me it was worth publishing.
Andy, your expertise, advice, and friendship
have changed my world.*

Acknowledgments

Alcoholics Anonymous: I have no words to express my gratitude for this wonderful, spiritual fellowship that not only saved my life but gave me a life, a spiritual do-over!

As always, Cole K. is my biggest fan, supporter, and partner in life. I thank you.

My dear friend Janet F. and I have been best buddies for more than forty precious years. Thank you for patiently listening to me read my stories to you for comments so many times.

Denise H., Oh my! How can I thank my friend who tirelessly offers the most insightful suggestions to help me write and rewrite?

Marilyn M., my wonderful and supportive friend who has a limitless ability to offer the most profound suggestions and has an unexpected talent for proofreading.

Renee O'H. – My partner in all things technical, including planning and organizing workshops. She does all the hard work! What more can I say?

The wonderful, patient, and honest women of my "focus" group. They listened to me read the book out loud and made suggestions; then we all went to our hangout, The Jellybird, for lunch! In alphabetical order, they are: Brenda, Carol, Dani, June, Karen, Linda, Mary Ellen, Renee, and Val – my heartfelt thanks to all of you.

Pamela Workman is an unexpected gift with extraordinary talents, patience, and knowledge of the publishing world.

Sarah Lahay's always beautiful and unique designs make the book shine!

Those brave Conference Chairmen – especially the wonderful Deric F., Sandy G., Dave B., and Chris P. – who asked me to present "The Rocking Chair" without knowing anything about it and not falling apart when I asked them for a rocking chair – *really!*

The tireless volunteers at Dr. Bob's Home, Wilson House, and Stepping Stones who are dedicated to preserving the landmarks of A.A. history. All proceeds from this book are donated to those three houses to help them in their efforts. A detailed description of the houses and what they represent is included in the back pages of this book.

Thank you to every person who has found something meaningful in my writing that will help them on their journey. Each of you obviously has an open mind and an open heart! My goal in life is to love and serve and to pass on the wisdom that was so freely given to me. Isn't it wonderful to know we are all links in this never-ending chain of sobriety?

Author's Note

A few years ago, my friend Deric invited me to speak at the annual Step Ashore Conference outside of Seattle, Washington. My topic was "The Principles Beneath the Principles." *What does that even mean?* As a writer, I began exploring my thoughts on paper, and by conference time, the story had blossomed into a very substantial manuscript.

I read it aloud to different groups of friends here at home. It was good. *I* liked what I had written. *They* liked what I had written.

I knew I couldn't just stand before the audience at the Conference and tell this story, and I didn't want to merely "read" it. I wanted to create an engaging *experience* for the audience.

Author's Note

Inspiration struck: I thought of my own front porch and the hours I spend in my rocking chair pondering and sharing the beauty and the challenges of life with other like-minded souls

I envisioned myself seated in a rocking chair on stage, wearing a long white dress, and sharing my narrative with those gathered together. And that is exactly what happened.

Thus was born "The Rocking Chair Book: Spirituality From My Front Porch."

Contents

Acknowledgments   i

Author's Note   v

Introduction   1

The Little Girl   3

The Beginning   9

The Story   11

"The God Thing"   13

"God as I understand Him"   15

Spiritual Awakening   18

Pondering Principles   20

Spiritual Experience   23

Carrying the Message   27

12 Step Calls   28

Principles   30

Faulty Childhood Principles   32

Manifestion of Old Ideas   36

Alcohol Arrives!   38

The Miracle   40

Alcoholics Anonymous?   41

Transformation   42

Healthy Principles / Healthy Repetition   44

Spiritual Disciplines   46

The Power of My Thoughts   47

Acting / Thinking / Feeling   49

Illusion of Separateness   52

Principle of Relatedness   54

Principle of Humility   56

Love and Service   58

Fellowship   61

Pain / Teachability / Love   63

Spiritual Connection   65

Action / Change   67

The Code   69

Realigning Principles   71

Suffering / Change   73

Practical Application 74

Addiction / Reading 78

Addiction / Alcohol 80

Drinking Story 82

The Miracle Happened 85

A.A. Journey 89

God's Schoolroom 90

Harmony 93

Three Houses 95

About the Author 99

Introduction

Why did I write this book?

In this lifetime, if we're lucky, we are able to share our universal stories of pain and rebirth with each other, and we are *both* enriched. We now have a spiritual bond. *I know you have been where I have been.* Maybe your road to hell was different than mine, but *how* we got there isn't the issue – the story of how we worked our way *out* of that hell – now ***that*** is the issue, and that is the story.

We are both the *hero* and the *villain* in our stories.

We have each engaged in our ordeal, our life-or-death crisis, during which we faced our greatest fears, our most difficult challenges, and emerged *triumphant* through hard work and spiritual change.

The hero's journey is a standard narrative in which a hero goes on an adventure, meets adversity, almost dies, learns a lesson, is changed, and returns home *transformed* to tell his story.

In *my* story, I was taken down into the depths of despair by a power outside myself that was more powerful than my own self-will or self-reliance. That abusive power was a bottle of alcohol! I was doomed.

But then the **miracle** happened, although at the time, I described it as "The worst day of my life."

What happened was this: a power greater than alcohol showed up as the *real* Hero (with a capital *H*) in my story. God, as I understand Him, is the *real* hero in my story. God showed up as a middle-aged, sober housewife. The encounter was life-changing.

Like most *human* heroes, I endured the pains of *resisting change* to emerge triumphant and happier than I could have ever imagined.

This is the story of that journey.

Hang on, hero – this can be *your* story, too!

The Little Girl

I want you to sit back, relax, and open your mind to a new experience. I'm going to tell you a story. If you were fortunate, as a child, someone read you a story at night before you went to sleep. If no one read to you *then*, I'm doing it *now*. I was lucky that way. Sometimes, I think my love of reading came from that simple bedtime story ritual.

I learned that all *good* stories start this way: **Once upon a time**.

So that's how I'll start:

Once upon a time, there was a little girl who grew up in a *moderately* crazy alcoholic family. She was a very pretty little girl, although she didn't think so. Inside, she felt she was a misfit;

she didn't really belong, but she *never* shared this with anyone. It was *her* secret.

Her parents described her this way: "She was a little girl, who had a little curl, right in the middle of her forehead. When she was good, she was very, very good, but when she was bad, she was horrid." (Henry Wadsworth Longfellow)

She, however, thought of herself as a princess as well as a horrid little girl.

And so she was — a little bit of both.

Her parents were completely self-reliant. They had money; they didn't need God. She believed that God was only a word, a sound, or a written symbol to be used by people who didn't have money.

So, as a child, she became completely self-reliant like her parents.

However, she was also restless, irritable, and discontented.

She was arrogant, anxious, insecure, resentful, unforgiving, and manipulative to the extreme. And *lonely*, so *lonely*.

That's one of the problems that come with being a Princess and a horrid little girl, unique and separate from everyone.

And so, because of her life experiences *and* her thinking, she concluded that other people were just cardboard cutouts on the stage she called her life, and *her* purpose in life was to control these cutouts so that she could always get her way. That was the way to happiness. After all, she was a horrid little girl princess!

To achieve her goal, she could be kind, patient, generous, considerate, even modest, and self-sacrificing.

On the other hand, she could be mean, selfish, egotistical, and dishonest.

She was fearfully self-centered — that was the root of her troubles, although she didn't think so. She truly believed that the problems in her life were all *your* fault! If you would only do as she wished, *everybody* would be happy!

When she grew up, she found that alcohol miraculously smoothed out the rough edges of her world and made her happy, so she drank more and more to be happier and happier.

One *horrible* day, she realized she could not stop drinking and stay stopped, and her world collapsed into pathetic, alcoholic despair.

She tried everything she could think of to moderate or control her drinking, but nothing worked.

Hopeless and broken, she *dragged* herself into the last house on the block, Alcoholics Anonymous.

She found it to be a *strange* place, full of light and love, but with the craziest "**suggestions**."

They said, "Here are *a group of principles,* **spiritual** in their nature, which, if practiced as *a way of life,* can expel the obsession to drink and enable the sufferer to become happily and usefully whole."

She said, "Obviously, there is a lot more to sobriety than not drinking."

They said, "The principles embedded in the Twelve Steps are **not** about how to stop *drinking.* They are about how to start *living.*

They are about learning to let go of faulty dependencies. They are about discovering love and tolerance of others. The world is a very beautiful and wonderful place. Life can be very easy when love becomes your way of life and when you see everything through the eyes of love."

"Okay Dokey," she said. "It is clear that *my* path to happiness doesn't work. I'm so miserable that I'm willing to go to any lengths to achieve the peace I seek. How do I grab onto these weird ideas."

"Oh, no," they said, *"You* can't do it. It takes a power much bigger than you." "How do I find this power?" she asked. "*Come on inside*, and we'll share *our* experience, strength, and hope with you along those lines. Welcome home."

And so she joined this new way of life. As the years passed, she painstakingly learned to put the principles of A.A. *inside* of her for the same reason she used to put *alcohol* inside of her - to feel better.

She was slowly transformed. She was changed from the self-centered little girl who came to A.A.

into a lovely, other-centered (and therefore God-centered) *grown-up woman.*

Healed in spirit, she was healed in her relationships with you, with *God*, even with *herself*. Motivated by this **spirit of love and tolerance**, she spent her life trying to live by these spiritual principles and to carry the message of these spiritual principles and spiritual perceptions to other alcoholics — and to everyone she met. She was a happy camper!

As she continued to practice *all* these principles on a daily basis, both inside and outside the rooms of Alcoholics Anonymous, she was at peace and lived reasonably happily ever after.

The end.

(I know you are surprised when I reveal that I am that little girl with a little curl right in the middle of her forehead. This is **my** story.)

The Beginning

I hope you liked my story about the little girl. I can't tell you how much fun I had writing it! It's called a *parable*. A parable is a story through which wisdom is passed, and our old ways of thinking are challenged.

I am a storyteller. It's what we do in Alcoholics Anonymous. It's in our story *telling* that we pass on life's lessons, and through story *hearing* that we connect what happens in our lives with the lessons in that happening. I wrote the story about the little girl with a little curl to illustrate the beautiful possibilities of *transformational change*. As I wrote that story, I began to think about the lessons I learned by incorporating the **Principles** of A.A. into my daily life. What about "The Principles *beneath* the Principles?" How monumental is that! What does that even mean? So, I wrote *a story* about what it might mean to me after nearly half a century of practicing these principles and the principles beneath the principles, in and outside the rooms of Alcoholics Anonymous. In sharing my story about principles, I'll also share with you what my life, my recovery, and my sobriety are all about.

Much to my initial dismay, I have recently admitted that I am also a teacher. I say "initial dismay" because I thought of a pompous, boring, stuffy *lecturer* when I thought of a teacher. I've been confronted with these people all my life and have discounted them as *judgmental spoilsports*. But then I thought, I am a teacher only because I have been taught by other teachers far wiser than I, who have shared their experience, strength, and hope with me over the years. They didn't *lecture* me; they *shared* with me, usually in the form of a story. *When one teaches, two learn. I am a link in a chain.*

The Story

When I was a newcomer to A.A., I heard that a very famous person was speaking at my Sunday night meeting. I arrived at the church *early*, pen and paper in hand, ready to take notes, and here's how this *very famous person* started his talk: "*I like cake*. I like cake with frosting between the layers. I like cake with frosting between the layers and lots of frosting on top. I like cake with frosting on the top and whipped cream and a *cherry* on the very top." He paused for a long time and then said, "And that's how I like my Alcoholics Anonymous. I WANT IT ALL, including the cherry on top."

I understood what he was saying!

His story set the tone for my A.A. I WANT IT ALL, including the cherry on top!

My journey of recovery started **not** by seeking new *landscapes* — we all know how well **that** works — it began by seeking a new way of looking at that landscape, a new pair of glasses. ***What I'm looking for, I'm looking with***. My **perspective** determines my **interpretation** of what I see. As a child, I came to believe that the world was a hostile, dangerous place, so that's what I looked for — a hostile universe, and that's what I found. In A.A., my attitude slowly changed as I stayed sober and worked the 12 Steps and 12 Traditions into my life. Today, I look for a loving universe, and that's what I find: a loving universe. What I'm looking for, I'm looking with.

I don't only share my knowledge; I share my *experience* and my *conclusions* about that experience.

"The God Thing"

Here is an example of what I mean. On the very *first* day of my sobriety, still wearing my dirty old nightgown with an untouched glass of Scotch beside me, I found myself on the phone with a stranger from A.A. I'll tell you more about her later, but here's the point I want to make: I was asked to look at what I called the *God thing* from an entirely different angle through a new pair of glasses. She suggested I ask God for help to stay sober for the remainder of a twenty-four period. I had a problem with that: my family did not raise me to believe in God; I was raised to think I could conquer anything using my willpower, strength, and self-reliance. Of course, I couldn't accomplish that task with alcohol; it didn't happen. In complete despair and hopelessness, I suffered a cumulative devastating defeat from alcohol and surrendered to my powerlessness. I was ripe for that phone call from this unknown woman. I was ripe for a new pair of glasses. Surprisingly, I did as this A.A. member suggested: I poured that glass of Scotch down the drain, got on my knees, and said an awkward prayer. Now that is willingness in action. What does willingness look like? It is me on my knees, **not** believing in God but following the directions of a stranger who had given me a little hope. That's willingness.

I haven't had a drink of alcohol since that day, October 16, 1975.

"God as I understand Him"

Through the spiritual experience of *physically* staying sober, I came to believe there is a power greater than my *self-reliance*. I came to call this power "God" because that is one of the agreed upon terms in the Western world for this power. *It's just a word*. It is just a sound or a written symbol, a speech sound that symbolizes and communicates a meaning. My friend Lori has a beautiful, practical explanation of God that I've adapted to fit me:

> *I believe there's only one God. I believe there is only one me.* My husband calls me sweetheart or honey. I have a daughter, and she calls me Mom. I have friends

who call me nicknames. All of them call me different names, and I have a different relationship with every one of them. There is no end to my love for each of them within that relationship. Every one of them is a *different* relationship. *But there's only one me.* And I think that's the way it is with God. I believe there is just one God. Some people call him Jesus, some call him Buddha, some call him Allah, some call him the moon and the stars, and some call him the spirit of nature. *It's just words* — speech sounds. We each have a different relationship with that Power, and how we get to that relationship is as unique and individual as every one of us.

That's what finally clicked for me and what works for me. The beauty of our A.A. program is that each of us believes whatever we want to believe, and no one can say we're wrong!

So, on that first day of sobriety, sick and shaking from alcoholic withdrawal, I started a relationship with God. I did that the same way I would do with anybody. I started talking to this "Higher Power." God speaks to me in a million ways. He talks to me through music; he talks to me through you, he talks to me through an overheard conversations at the next table, a book I'm reading, the birds singing early in the morning, the moon rising at night — *if I'm tuned in, I hear him.*

Over the years, we have developed quite a wonderful relationship.

So now you understand the context in which I speak of "God." Nothing personal — no axe to grind — just an acknowledged power that is bigger than I am — bigger than the great I AM!!

Spiritual Awakening?

Through my teachers, I am traveling from *unknowing* ignorance to the *experiential unfolding* of my life. The funny thing is that I am aware that most of you know the conclusions I'm going to write about. I also know that we have each had the **same spiritual awakening**. By this, I mean that we have each had our own AHA! moment, a ***five-second shift in perception*** that resulted in a different angle of approach.

My spiritual awakening was as unique to me as yours was to you. Bill Wilson had his *own* spiritual awakening, and it was unique to him. Only in A.A. do we continue to peel this onion over and over again, reaching ever-deepening AHA! moments and delighting in the discoveries! Then, we share them and find that *we are all connected*.

A.A. *reinvents* itself with *every* newcomer and with *every* spiritual awakening.

To have the experience, I have to have *lived* it. *I can't explain it*, but I can tell you it's true because I have *experienced* it in Alcoholics Anonymous. Through sharing our mutual experiences, we are loved back into the one tribe we belong to, the one we have yearned for. There is no "me." There is no "they." "*We*" are "they." *We are each other.*

Pondering Principles

So, among other things, I'm an alcoholic, I'm a writer, I'm a reader, and I'm a teacher. I also ponder. *I think about things.* I looked up "ponder" in the dictionary: "to consider something deeply and thoroughly."

I think about the principles the little girl practiced which transformed her. "The principles beneath the principles," or "practice these principles." What exactly does this mean? I have no idea. But I am excited — something new to ponder.

In Alcoholics Anonymous, I've discovered that until I can *define* a problem, I can't recognize a *solution* when it arrives. I've also learned that *when in doubt, start at the beginning.*

So, I start at the beginning. "We practice these principles in all our affairs." What is a *principle*?

*PRINCIPLE is from a Latin word meaning FIRST. It is a fundamental truth that forms the foundation on which other things are built **and** which governs their operation.*

Principles are the *first* things that come *before* on which *other* things rest.

Principles are *objective, universal,* and *permanent. The Principles in A.A. are spiritual in nature.*

The message is clear throughout our A.A. literature: we must seek and utilize a Power greater than ourselves to live happy, useful, alcohol-free lives. ***Then we have to do a bunch of other things.***

Look at the ***actions*** in the Steps. *These are actions, not passive beliefs.* We must admit powerlessness, take inventory, confess our mistakes, make amends, continue taking inventory, and carry the message. *But these actions are NOT Principles.* The Principles are at the ***root*** of these actions.

THE TWELVE STEPS ARE THE TOOLS THAT MANIFEST THE PRINCIPLES. *The Steps are guides to action that open the doors and activate the Principles within us.*

In other words, the Steps unlock the doors so the God within me can work without me!

For example, *one* of the Principles in the First Step is surrender, the action it requires is to admit complete defeat and powerlessness. However, sometimes each Step involves the practice of more than one Principle, and some of the same principles are involved in more than one Step. While surrender is *one* of the Principles embedded in the First Step, so is the Principle of open-mindedness. And how about humility?

How well we work the Steps depends entirely on how well we practice the PRINCIPLES embedded in them.

This seems like such a no-brainer. But it doesn't tell me much that I can translate into *me, me, me!*

Spiritual Experience

So I look again at our literature: "A.A.'s Twelve Steps are a group of Principles, *spiritual in their nature*, which, if practiced as a way of life, can expel the obsession to drink and enable the sufferer to become happily and usefully whole." (Forward to the Twelve Steps and Twelve Traditions.)

When I first came to A.A., I *knew* that not drinking was *not* enough. I had *tried* not drinking off and on for *three long years* before I *surrendered* and admitted complete defeat. I was told I have an illness that is physical, emotional, and spiritual; therefore, I must take specific steps to heal in all three areas of my life. I was told that to "*thoroughly follow the path*," I had to have a significant change *inside of me.* This IS a spiritual awakening. I recover first spiritually, then physically and emotionally. I argued with my sponsor about this sequence of events: "Hey, I stopped drinking *first*." She pointed out that I had to exercise the *spiritual Principles* of surrender, humility, and willingness in order to admit complete defeat (powerlessness) and ask for help from a source outside myself. *Then,* I was able to stop drinking. She said I could count this admission as a **spiritual experience.**

What is a spiritual experience?

In the appendix of our textbook, *Alcoholics Anonymous*, a spiritual experience is defined as "A personality change sufficient to bring about recovery from alcoholism — **a profound alteration in my reaction to life**." Such a change could hardly have been brought about by myself alone.

I have tapped into an inner resource that I presently identify with my *own* conception of a Power greater than myself. **This *awareness* of a Power greater than myself is the essence of a spiritual experience.**

Remember the misplaced phone call I mentioned before? I had my *first* spiritual experience pertaining to sobriety the day I admitted my powerlessness over alcohol to that sober member of Alcoholics Anonymous, asked for her help, and, most importantly, *followed her suggestions.*

Listening to her talk about *her* feelings about herself, *her* drinking, and *her* recovery, I moved from hopelessness to hope. I began to think, "If I do what she does, maybe I can feel the way she feels."

I believe spiritual experiences are cumulative, sequential, and progressive, just like my alcoholism is cumulative, sequential, and progressive. Each Alcoholics Anonymous *generation* has to make its own discoveries of Spirit. No one can make the journey for us.

Since my last drink in October of 1975, my spiritual experiences have been like **popcorn popping** — you know what that's like — at first, there is no sound, then a little *pop*, then two more *pops*, then rapid-fire popping, *pop, pop, pop, pop,*

pop, which supposedly slows down to an occasion-al *pop*, *pop*. It hasn't slowed down for me yet. I'm not done! *If anything, it's increased in intensity over the last few years. Today's popping* is still as life-changing and exciting as that first pop!

Carrying the Message

The Twelfth Step concludes that we've had a spiritual experience as THE result of these Steps. It further states that we must try to carry this message to others and practice all these principles in all our affairs. What is this message? My message is that I have had a spiritual awakening that has transformed me and changed my whole attitude and outlook toward life, toward my fellows, toward myself, and toward God. How do I carry this message? I incorporate and *live* these principles in my daily life through the example I represent and through sharing my personal experiences — my story.

12 Step Calls

When I was newly sober, my sponsor called me one day and said, "We're going on a 12-step call. I'll pick you up in 20 minutes." In the car, she explained that a lady had called A.A.'s Central Office and asked for help with her drinking. The 12th Step of Alcoholics Anonymous says, *"Having had a spiritual awakening as the result of these Steps, we tried to carry this message to alcoholics and to practice these principles in all our affairs."* We've already established that I had a spiritual experience just before getting sober, so our 12-step job was to visit her, share with her the nature of alcoholism, **and** tell her what happened to us — our spiritual experience.

"I have nothing to say," I whined (it was all about me, of course.) "Rena, she will believe you because she can imagine not drinking for three *weeks*. She can't imagine being sober for the number of *years* I have." "Besides," she said, "If she *wants* to get sober, nothing you can say will be wrong. If she *doesn't* want to get sober, there's nothing you can say that will be right. *Our job is simply to show up!*" So we visited that lady. I couldn't believe how excited I was to share the **wonder** of being sober. I found myself wanting the *best* for this woman, with no strings attached. I felt love flowing **out of me** for the first time in my life. Love in the past had always been, "What can you do for me that shows me how much you love me, me, me?" My sponsor later said that I **showed** that woman the miracle of sobriety; I didn't just **talk** about it. I *demonstrated* the Principles of humility, love, and service. I showed up. And that *is* the message!

Principles

And the PRINCIPLES?

I'm going to try to share with you my experience and my personal interpretation of both this message and these principles. Remember, this is just my understanding at this moment in my life. You probably have figured out all this stuff a long time ago, but this is where I am with it. My interpretation will grow and change as I continue to grow and change. (I could not have had these insights ten years ago; I will probably chuckle about them ten years from now).

When I was about six months sober, I was handed a little card on which was printed each Step and presumably its corresponding *one and only* Principle. Being new, I took this literally, *clinging* to these definitions as *Absolute Truths.*

The card said the *Principle* of the First Step was "honesty." It seemed to require no action on my part, and presumably, it was the only principle involved.

Many years later, when pondering the Principles of Alcoholics Anonymous, I began to think about that card, its rigid little Principles, and the concept of Principles in my personal life.

I had an "AHA!" moment when it began to dawn on me that **this was nothing new: I had always practiced Principles in my life**, *but they were faulty, stressful, and ineffective.*

Faulty Childhood Principles

I was raised in a military family: father, mother, me, little brother, little sister. As a result of the military, we moved *all the time*. I never spent one year in one school until high school. I have no memory of ever feeling okay. A line in the Twelve & Twelve talks about "*anxious apartness,*" which completely describes how I felt. Somehow, I felt unloved, unworthy, and fearful: "Something is wrong with me; nobody likes me, I'm different, I don't belong." To illustrate how my "ISM" is *inside* of me, let me tell you that my brother and sister were happy all the time and *loved* to move and meet new people, while I absolutely hated my life.

When I was seven, my little brother died suddenly and unexpectedly. He was five years old. *My parents never mentioned him again, at least in my presence.* I can't even imagine how they felt. They were from an era that never talked about anything, much less their *feelings*. There is no criticism here; it's just how it was in those days. I believe my mother also died that day. She became emotionally disconnected, and of course, I took it personally.

Something *big* shifted in me. I set up walls between me and everyone. I know *now* that I didn't know *how* to *feel my feelings* and was terrified to face the awful *reality* of what had happened to my little brother and what might happen to *me* that *I couldn't control.* Maybe this is where my ever-present feelings of "anxious apartness" accelerated. The parents I had believed were *all-powerful* could not protect *me* any more than they could save my little brother.

So I pretended. As a frightened child, I **consciously** became something I was not. I developed my own strategy for managing *my* world, out-wardly appearing *defiantly self-reliant,* which manifested as a hostile arrogance.

I was seven years old!

I was unaware that my **self-centered fear** *was the basis of my orientation to life.* The **Principle** was self-centered fear; my **manifestation of self-reliance** *rested* on that foundation of fear, my way of processing the world around me. This led to an emotional isolation and loneliness I carried into adulthood and into the rooms of Alcoholics Anonymous.

I lived as a reactionary. I lived *in reaction* to instincts, emotions, and impulsive desires dis-guised as **needs** — *all fueled by my own frightened self-will,* my way of processing the world around me. What we are feeling *inside* of us colors our world.

The *fear* that controlled my life, my choices, and my decisions led to the formation of the character defects of dishonesty, intolerance, and self-seeking. Defective as they were, the *conclusions* I reached about how to navigate my life successfully became *my* guiding Principles.

Manifestation of Old Ideas

Here are some of the **manifestations** *of those Principles:* I must control and manipulate others to get what I want. I *con* you into believing I am competent. I hide my vulnerability because I define it as a weakness. I never ask for anything *openly*; if I do, I risk refusal because *you* know I'm not worthy. Instead, I manipulate to control.

Through the Steps, I found that these attitudes were set in stone when I was just a seven-year-old child. In A.A., I learned to name most of them "character defects," "old ideas," and "the exact nature of my wrongs." My little bag of tricks was full of *negative*, deeply ingrained habits, strengthened by ***repeated*** actions to calm my *self-centered fear*. I felt safe behind the barriers I had built.

Alcohol Arrives!

Then came alcohol! For a while, it was my answer to the problem of life; then, it became the problem. *Alcohol gave me wings to fly, and then it took away the sky.* One night, during that terrible three-year period when I believed my willpower alone would give me the power to control my drinking, I experienced the terrible gut-level *awareness* that **alcohol owned me**, and I would never, *ever* recapture the magic feeling of that first drink. I had no power. This was ***not intellectual knowledge; it*** was *visceral*. I had been told for years that if I continued to drink, I would die; these warnings went into my head and lodged there, only adding to my despair. **I surrendered to this powerlessness and continued to drink**.

I couldn't see life with or without alcohol. I was doomed.

The Miracle

Before I could successfully quit my alcoholic, compulsive drinking, I had to *experience* a sufficient reason to stop. I needed a miracle!

And then the **miracle** happened. Earlier, I wrote about the woman who called me by mistake on *October 16, 1975*. Because of that *misplaced* phone call and a conversation with a woman I didn't know, who just happened to call me, and who just happened to have six years in Alcoholics Anonymous, I *experienced* a sudden shift in my perception. I became willing to surrender my will *momentarily* to follow someone else's direction. *That shift in perception is also known as a spiritual awakening.* **It changed my life!**

Alcoholics Anonymous?

Coming into A.A., I was told that alcohol was just a *symptom* of what was wrong with me. Self-centeredness was my basic problem, and the only solution to that problem was spiritual. Once I had put down the drink, *I had to change.* "Change what?" I asked. "Change everything," you said. "Ok," I said. "Where do I start?" "Oh, *you* can't make these changes," you said. "You have no power. Only a Power bigger than you can do the job." I had *already* conceded to my innermost self that I was powerless over *alcohol.* Does this mean I'm powerless over *everything?*

Pretty much!

Transformation

I was told that the Steps of Alcoholics Anonymous were *universal truths* that allowed me to step out, *so to speak*, from my *tiny* box of *self-centered fear* into the ever-expanding *sunlight of the spirit*. I suffered from a spiritual malady, a soul sickness, an *illusion* of control that **I created myself**. I desperately needed a TRANSFORMATION. My favorite definition of transformation is "**change without effort on my part**." Transformation is different from acquiring facts and information. *Information* inflates my ego; *transformation* humbles it. My personal transformation was this: as the overall result of these Steps, I have had a spiritual awakening. I have *been* changed. That **is** the "message." I have found a loving God who saved me from my thinking and who can do the same for *others if he is sought*. I have found a certain degree of *detachment* from my own **emotional narcissism**. Oh, could I write a book about *that*: **emotional narcissism**!

Healthy Principles / Healthy Repetition

As I internalize and practice our recovery program — these Principles — the *power of repetition* reveals *new* Principles. I accumulated fresh, new, positive habits. *I have to do to be.* I am what I repeatedly **do**, not what I repeatedly **think**. By *continuously* repeating the **actions** of **healthy** Principles, I begin to live in the solution. I stand at a turning point a *thousand* times a day, and **my *next* step determines the direction of my path:** am I moving towards a drink or away from a drink? "Alcohol is a subtle foe," it says in our Big Book. It could also have said "and patient."

Through the actions of **continuous** surrender, I have to let go of the story *I* created, the one I've made up. I have been *reacting* all my life to my own story, which wasn't even true!

Spiritual Disciplines

Principles are the foundation of spiritual work. Doing and becoming, doing and becoming, is the way I grow away from a negative, self-centered habitual way of thinking to a positive, other-centered, God-oriented life. *Internal* peace. The principles of Alcoholics Anonymous as spiritual disciplines are guides to spiritual progress, enabling us to grow away from mere physical sobriety to emotional sobriety and emotional maturity.

Psychiatrists have labeled alcoholics as "immature, sensitive, and grandiose." It takes some of us a long time to get over it!

The Power of My Thoughts

I believe no child is born feeling unloved, unworthy, or fearful. No child is born feeling "Something is wrong with me, nobody likes me, I'm different, I don't belong." And yet, this was my core belief about myself as a little girl. No one told me this; it was *my* perception. It was the conclusion I drew about me, about you, and about *life*. As a result of this *weltanschauung*, this worldview, I devised my **own** ways of coping with life.

The Big Book says, "We suffered under the *delusion* that we could *wrest* satisfaction and happiness out of this world if we could only *manage* well."

Buddha says: "Our life is shaped by our mind, for we become what we think."

Our Big Book also says, *"Our trouble centers in our minds rather than our bodies."* It advises us: *"On awakening, we ask God to direct our **thinking**."* *I came here because of my **drinking**; I **stay** here because of my **thinking**.*

*I could talk forever about the **power** of my thoughts.* Before A.A., my thoughts were a *constant*, never-ending stream of **judgments** and **opinions** which create **feelings** about those judgments, which create the actions I take based on those thoughts. WOW! My *judgmental thinking* ruled my life! So, if my **thinking** is unhealthy, my **actions** will be unhealthy. *I say that judgment is a value system partnered with my past experiences.* I am simply the listener; **I** don't create the thoughts. I am not my thoughts, but I'm *powerless* over thinking them.

Acting / Thinking / Feeling

In A.A., I found out that by *repeatedly* changing my **actions,** my thoughts and feelings would **change**. I grew up believing I had to sit down and "figure things out" and maybe take action based on my *feelings* about those *thoughts*. I really believed my *permission* was needed. **I was filled with faulty thinking and limiting beliefs.** Imagine my surprise when I finally "figured out" that life didn't need *my* stamp of approval for it to happen. I was told that "Figuring things out" is not an A.A. slogan!

Let me give you an example of how **changing my actions changed my thinking and feeling**.

Three weeks sober, I found myself financially broke and moving in with my widowed father. *Oh, the humiliation!* One day my thinking went down a familiar rabbit hole of *negative arrogance*: "I'm a grown-up living with my father. What a *loser* I am. I've always been a loser, but it's not my fault. If only so and so hadn't — *fill in the blank* — abandoned me, not abandoned me, **whatever.** I wouldn't be in this situation if they had treated me right. *It's not fair.* It's always been this way; it will always be this way. I might as well give up — *what's the use?* Why bother? Poor me, poor me! Pour me a drink!" Then I would reach for the Scotch bottle. It was all about me, me, me!

But not this time. As I was going through my pitiful, familiar litany, a voice came into my head. It said, "What are you going to do about it TODAY?" I was startled. "Oh my, I guess I could get in my car and find an A.A. meeting for tonight." *And so I did.* I immediately *felt* better as I left my father's house. I *did* find that meeting. *I stood at a turning point. I took a healthy action, and* *healthy thoughts and feelings followed*. Of course, I was unaware of what had happened and could not have articulated it even if I had known.

At a meeting a few weeks later, I heard a speaker say: "**I have to act my way into good thinking; I can't think my way into good acting.**"

Profound. I wrote it down. It became the **foundation** of my sober life, my *go-to direction* for what to do next. Sometimes, the next right action is just to brush my teeth and go to bed. *God* will be up all night anyway, so I don't have to stay awake and worry. *Worry is just low-grade atheism*. Think about it.

Illusion of Separateness

*The root of my trouble IS self-centeredness. One of its **manifestations** is the illusion of **separateness**.* From early childhood, I felt separated from you, from a God I didn't believe in, and even from me! I was in this universe alone and defenseless. I believe that is where my orientation of self-centered fear comes from. In A.A., when I was finally able to become really honest with my hostile, deranged self, I came to believe that I had nothing to *prove*, nothing to *protect*, nothing to *defend*. I came to believe that my sense of disconnection was self-delusional and self-inflicted. It was an illusion I made up! In reality, I connect with everything and everyone — *everything* belongs. I BELONG. When I am in tune with my inner connection rather than separateness, the results are real, true, and beautiful. It stands to reason that if I am a child of God and *I* belong, then every person is a child of God, and every person belongs. This is true whether I like the person or not!

As I use the language of the heart, my connectedness grows. *My inner and my outer world are unified.* A friend said to me one day, "Rena, you are the same person with *everybody.*" Because of my experiences in A.A., I am able to know *me* and to be who *I* am. I am able to pass along the wisdom of all the teachers I've had along the way. The best part of sharing *their* wisdom is that I get to hear what I say, and I hear *their* voices. I have no idea what *you* hear unless I ask you and you tell me.

All right, back to Principles.

Principle of Relatedness

Here's one for you to ponder: ***RELATEDNESS*** *as the unifying principle of the Universe.*

Let me tell you what I mean. All of these principles indicate *involvement with God, involvement with you, and even involvement with **me**.* This points to some kind of *relatedness* to the Universe.

Let's examine this premise. I used to be one of those awful students who liked to *diagram sentences.* Remember that in grade school?

Today, if I were to diagram a sentence about Alcoholics Anonymous, it would look like this:

GOD (LOVE)

HUMILITY

Honesty. Purity. Unselfishness. Love.
Consideration. Integrity. Faith.
Compassion. Open-mindedness.
Kindness. Courtesy. Respect.
Responsibility. Trust. Accountability.
Balance. Clarity. Empathy.

Every one of those Principles indicates a *re-lationship*. All of the Principles listed above have a **subject** and an **object**. Let's look at some of the Principles on that list, and you'll see what I mean. **Surrender** — to what? **Tolerance** — of what? **Forgiveness** — of what and to whom? **Compassion**, *Courtesy, Faith* — all these principles indicate a *relationship* to something or someone. *We don't practice principles in a vacuum*! We **can't** practice principles in a vacuum. *Here's an idea* — make your *own* list of the principles that are important to you and see how each principle involves a **relationship**, no matter how lengthy or fleeting.

Principle of Humility

Here's another revelation for you. These are just *some* of the Principles beneath the ***Primary Principle of HUMILITY. All of A.A.'s principles are based on humility***. And what is humility? Our Big Book talks about humility as ***the desire to seek and do God's Will***. Humility is *awareness* of my powerlessness, my own *illusion* of control. It's *surrender* and *reliance on God*. It's right-sizing me. It's ***teachability***. It's the *Serenity Prayer*. I have come to believe that ***the Principle of Humility is the foundation of each of the 12 Steps and 12 Traditions, and of our whole program! That's a big deal.***

"Hi, I'm Rena, and I'm an alcoholic," is a humble and honest admission of reality. Alcoholics Anonymous teaches me that I don't come to God by doing life right; I come to God by doing it wrong and then falling into an infinite mercy A.A. calls "Higher Power." God does not love me because *I* am good; God loves me because **God** is good. I read that somewhere and it brings me comfort.

Love and Service

Love and Service are the core of Alcoholics Anonymous. **Beneath** the Principles of Love and Service is the Principle of *humility*. Humility paves the way to the spiritual awakening we must have in order to overcome drinking. God is love, and love is humble.

If God is love and I come from God, isn't that the purpose of it all? "Deep down in every man, woman, and child is the fundamental idea of God." Isn't that humility? Isn't that the Principle from which all others flow?

I think the humble act of one drunk unselfishly helping another drunk encompasses *all* of the Principles of Alcoholics Anonymous. Our salvation, our program, and our fellowship began with one drunk, sober six months, telling his story to a drinking drunk who wanted to be sober and didn't know how. Our Big Book says, "In spite of the great increase in the size and span of this fellowship, at its core, it remains simple and personal. Each day, somewhere in the world, recovery begins when one alcoholic talks to another alcoholic, sharing his experience strength and hope." "A.A.'s speak the language of the heart in all its power and simplicity."

I came here because of me — I stay here because of us.

You tell my story over and over, and I realize I'm not the only one. All my life, I have felt separate, alone, and *overwhelmingly lonely*. It turns out that was a lie I told myself at seven years old in an effort to protect myself from... *from what*? From some awful, secret, *imagined* fear of impending doom.

So I'm saying I have come to believe that God is *oneness* and *harmony*. GOD IS RELATEDNESS. *God is unity*. **Unity is not the same as uniformity**.

Unity is the reconciliation of differences. If we are in unity with the Spirit, then we are in unity with each other. Every person is bound to every other person in a *reciprocal* relationship.

And so we are all one. When I look deeply into you, I find me. *Humility is the recognition of the Spirit of God as the unifying Principle of all life, and it becomes the most important experience I can ever have.*

Fellowship

Here's another word for what I experience in recovery: FELLOWSHIP. Fellowship is a kind of belonging that is based on a deep belief that everyone matters, everyone is welcome, and everyone is loved—in other words, — humility.

Julian of Norwich, one of my favorite mystics, said, "The love of God creates in us such a ONEING that when it is truly seen, no person can separate themselves from another person." (Revelations of Divine Love)

Chuck C. says, "There is only one problem which includes all problems and only one solution which includes all solutions. The only problem in life is a *conscious* separation from

God; the only solution is a *connection* to God."
(A New Pair of Glasses)

I grew up feeling a conscious separation from **everything**. I existed separate from **everything**.

What is the problem? All my life, I was looking *outside* of myself for a solution to a problem that is *inside*. What is the solution? What is the answer to the problem inside? What is the problem again? **A God-shaped hole.** How do I get from the problem to the solution? By putting the Principles embedded in the Twelve Steps *inside* of me just as I used to put alcohol *inside* of me — *to feel better!* Self-centeredness and humility are completely opposite orientations toward life. How do I get from one attitude to the other? Sometimes by *prayer,* sometimes by *pain.*

Pain / Teachability / Love

They say *pain* is the touchstone of spiritual growth. One of my favorite poets, Anais Nin, wrote: "*And the day came when the risk to remain tight in a bud was more painful than the risk it took to blossom.*"

How I cling to the familiar. I look back and see how impossible *any* change appears beforehand and how simple and freeing it appears *afterward*.

Look at our drinking. When the *pain* of continuing to drink became greater than the *pain* of **not** drinking, we asked for help, and the drinking stopped. **We became teachable**.

Saint Francis says: "Lord, make me a channel of thy peace; that I may bring love, comfort, and understanding to others."

"Namaste" means: "The Spirit in me recognizes and salutes the Spirit in you."

Don M. says, "When living in love, I am living in God's Magic. When I behave lovingly, I believe I begin to bear a slight resemblance to my Creator." (Stumbling in the Right Direction)

They all teach the same *eternal* message, the universal message of love.

Our journey is beautiful. We don't do it alone. We **can't** do it alone. "*Without Him, I can't; without me, He won't.*"

Spiritual Connection

The other morning, I was driving to my 8 AM home group meeting. It was a wonderful Florida morning, sunny and warm. I passed a lot of people walking their dogs, living their lives. I got a lump in my throat, and tears began to fall. **I suddenly felt so *connected*.** I am part of this whole. I belong. We're all in this together. Sometimes, that connection is almost *painful; it* is so intense. It can only be felt in the moment, in the NOW. God is in that moment. I'm suddenly aware of how *precious* and fleeting everything is. I felt JOY — that elusive, *transitory moment* when everything becomes one, and *everything* is just as it should be. For just that moment, *I saw the big picture*. I once asked my sponsor why I couldn't just crawl into moments like that and live there. "You would soon take it for granted," she said. "It would no longer hold the importance it does when it's fleeting."

"God is everything, or He is nothing." God is Everything, but there's also ME. I've come to believe that I'm just *part* of that Everything.

Action / Change

Okay, so I've gotten WAY ahead of myself! These thoughts are probably something I should share later when I'm ready to wrap up my time with you. However, this is how it's revealing itself to me and, therefore, to you.

Let me back up a little. I told you that I was about three weeks sober when I heard a speaker say, **"I have to act my way into good thinking; I can't think my way into good acting."** I had no idea what it meant, but I felt it was important, so I wrote it down. I wrote down everything important in those days because I thought I had drunk my way into a wet brain — I couldn't remember *anything*.

This statement implied that I must take action to change my thinking — my bad thinking habits. I had to develop new habits based on the principles of A.A. In the beginning, this meant the actions I took were just going to meetings and trying to be a nice person. *Pretty good for a newcomer!* Since then this statement has become the foundation of my program, together with our code. All right, I'll bite: *What is our code?*

The Code

My sponsor called me one day and asked, "Did you know A.A. has a code?" "No," I replied, "What is it?" "It's in the Big Book — you'll find it." CLICK. It took *three* readings of the first 164 because I kept getting lost in the book, but I finally found it. "LOVE AND TOLERANCE *OF OTHERS* IS OUR CODE." Now, I play the same prank on others! I do not give away the page number!

Here is the whole enchilada in one sentence. *My A.A. program is based on the Principles of love, service, and tolerance of others, which is achieved by changing my negative thinking and feeling through* repetitively *changing my behavior.*

In other words, I must incorporate the PRINCIPLES and the PRINCIPLES BENEATH THOSE PRINCIPLES embedded in the Twelve Steps into my very being on a daily, minute-to-minute basis. This is sometimes a daunting task.

Realigning Principles

My ego *screams* at such perceived humiliation! But it really **is** just about ***realigning** the Principles of faith and trust*. After all, as a child, I had **faith** in the ugly story I told myself *about* myself and **trusted** in its truth. I *lived* by that story. I made *life decisions* based on that story. ***It was MY story!***

My sponsor pointed out that I had faith and trust in ***alcohol*** until I didn't. Again, I had to realign my belief system.

If you remember, I was told at the beginning that *I* couldn't make the changes — only in partnership with my Higher Power can these changes be made. *Without Him, I can't; without me, He won't.* I've been trying to do my part for almost half a century, day in and day out, and still don't get it right some days. But I'm better today than I was a year ago or ten years ago! This is one reason A.A. never gets boring. How can I get complacent when I'm constantly learning about **me, me, me**?

Suffering / Change

This ability to change is often the result of *suffering*. Suffering is "**whenever we feel we're not in control**." *"Lack of power, that is our dilemma."* One of the most powerful sentences in the Big Book is this: *"We **suffered** under the delusion that we could wrest satisfaction and happiness out of this world if we only managed well."* I looked up the word "**wrest**." It means "to seize with force." The first time I read this, I realized this was ME — this was ME *all my life.*

Kind of crazy, isn't it? But that's what we do — until we don't.

Practical Application

WHAT DOES THIS ALL MEAN? How does this translate into *practicality?*

Here's an example: *newly sober*, I was in the bank waiting in line to cash a check. I found myself getting irritated. I thought, "Don't they know who I am?" "I have things to do?" Suddenly, this voice came into my head: "***Practice these principles in all our affairs.***" *Even in the bank?* Yes, even in the bank. Instead of walking out of the bank in self-defeating disgust ("I'll show you, I'll hurt me!"), I changed my ***behavior*** by taking a deep breath and talking with the woman in line in front of me. *She* was a little irritated, too, and we had a nice conversation! My thinking changed because I changed my behavior, and as a bonus, I found another small connection to humanity.

I was learning to practice Patience, one of those elusive Principles *beneath* the Principle of Humility.

The first joke I heard in A.A. was about Humility. It took me years to understand what the joke was about. *Here it is:* a man was voted the most humble person in his town and was given a pin with "Most Humble Person in this Town" inscribed on it. As soon as he pinned it on himself, they took it away from him!

The definition of humility I like best is this: *the desire to seek and do God's Will.* The only knowledge I have of God's Will for me is in the spiritual 4th dimension of RIGHT NOW. "There is One who has all power; that One is God. May you find him — (When? Where?) — **NOW.**"

"Relieve me of the bondage of self," we ask in the 3rd step prayer. ***This is one of the most powerful concepts in the Big Book***. The *significance* of the "bondage of self" will continue to unfold for the rest of my life in order to maintain my spiritual fitness. And the reason we pray for relief from this self-obsessed, fear-based orientation? So that we may better do *His* Will and be of service to others. Over the years, that prayer has changed in meaning as I have gained insight into the **root of my troubles**. I had spent my life hiding from the message I told myself as a child: *I am not enough.* As a result of this faulty belief about myself, I consciously separated myself from you so you wouldn't know and I wouldn't have to see it and put the blame on you. I was a victim — *a spectator in my own life.* I devised compensatory strategies to deal with life: trying to satisfy my needs for security, approval, and power. There was a deep drive in me to find happiness, but I was always looking *outside of me* for fulfillment: The new car, the new dress, the new man, the *other* new man, *your approval,* the move to another city, state, or country.

As a child, my perceptions, judgments, and conclusions about the world had solidified into the person I later dragged into A.A. I needed a drink by the time I was seven, but I settled for my first addiction, ***reading***.

Addiction / Reading

My favorite definition of addiction is this: addiction is a distraction from intolerable reality. Sometimes the "intolerable reality" is inside of us, in our thoughts and feelings.

When my little brother died, I already knew how to read, but now I dove right in and **lived** in my books. I always thought I read to escape, but looking back on *what* I read, I was drawn to books about happy families who worked together, played together, and loved each other. They even *prayed* together, a foreign concept in my family. There was a sense of belonging in those families that I yearned for. I was so lonely.

Many years later in A.A., I discovered that the empty hole in me was God-shaped, which meant it was also **you**- shaped and **me**- shaped. At seven years old, I had completely separated myself from everything and was totally self-reliant. "If it is to be, it is up to me." I developed my own set of rules about right and wrong, good and bad, and I clung to them as rigidly as if they were a lifeboat and I would drown if I didn't hold on. To me, the world was a stormy, scary, dark sea, and I was in it alone.

Addiction / Alcohol

This was the woman I brought to my *first* drink of alcohol. I was on a date, and I was nervous. I took that first drink **to change my feelings,** to take away the fear, and oh, boy, did it! I know every alcoholic understands what I'm talking about. Alcohol fixed something in me that needed fixing. **For the first time in my whole life,** *I relaxed*.

Alcohol brought me freedom from ME. Alcohol brought me freedom from that awful anxious apartness I'd felt my whole life. I believe I was an alcoholic from that first drink because I couldn't control the amount I drank right from the get-go. I had intended to have *one* drink and ended up drunk. Looking back, I realize I did this *every time* I drank. **"Alcohol gave me wings to fly, and then it took away the sky."**

I knew nothing about alcoholism. I knew nothing about the disease of alcoholism or of its progressive nature. It's cunning, baffling, and powerful that way

"The chains of alcoholism are too weak to be felt until they are too strong to be broken."

So I lived my life knowing very little but thinking I knew everything!

Drinking Story

I really believe I live my life on at least two levels: the outside one where I go to school, get married, travel, work, etc. On a deeper level, I'm living symbolically, where the inner pressure is felt.

On the outside level, I drank more, and I drank more often; I didn't drink if I could only have one. I gave up my friends and social gatherings because I didn't want to appear drunk in front of people. I began to drink at home, alone at night, reading or watching television. I began to drink earlier in the day. I started to drink in the morning. I was alone and completely isolated.

In 1972, I went to one A.A. meeting in Dallas, Texas. I was so drunk that I remember nothing about the meeting, but *I do* remember arrogantly thinking as I drove away, "Isn't it nice *those people* have a place to go." I knew that with my trusty *self-reliance,* I could control the situation. But just in case "those people" followed me, I packed my car the next day and moved to Florida. I didn't know it then, but I would spend the next *three years* in *vain* attempts to moderate or quit drinking alcohol. It was a full-time job. It was a living hell.

On a typical day between 1972 and 1975, when I awoke, I would be *shaking* because of alcohol withdrawal; I learned that a glass of Scotch would help me avoid vomiting and calm my nerves, so I would get my Scotch and get back in bed. There was no cable, internet, or streaming in those days, so I'd watch Captain Kangaroo on TV and feel sorry for myself because the world and its people weren't treating me right. The days were *very* long and boring. I would take a "nap," come to, and start *all over again*. In despair and longing, I clung to my *right to drink*. I lived in my ratty old nightgown, didn't have the energy to take a shower or wash my hair, didn't eat, and just existed to drink alcohol. Once in a while, I would stop drinking because *I felt I was losing control!!* If I hadn't put myself in a hospital first, I would have been in serious trouble because I would have seizures — convulsions — from withdrawal. I was so alone and lonely, although I was the one who had run everybody off. The pain was unbearable.

This was my life at 7:30 AM on October 16, 1975.

The Miracle Happened

And then the miracle happened!

The phone rang. My phone never rang. I had pushed away everyone in my life in order to safeguard my right to drink. I answered it. On the phone was a woman I didn't know, who didn't know me; she had gotten my number by mistake. Somehow, the subject of drinking came up. It turns out she was six years sober in Alcoholics Anonymous. We talked on that phone all day.

Now, I have seen psychiatrists and other counselors over the years, and they always said, "Tell me about yourself." This woman said, *"Let me tell you about me."* The power of identification is monumental! It's the divine spark, the connection that made A.A. possible when Dr. Bob Smith met and *identified* with Bill Wilson in 1935. Forty years later, the woman on the phone told me about *her* drinking and *her* feelings of loneliness, shame, and guilt. She talked about *her* inability to stop drinking and stay stopped, *her* surrender, and *her* recovery. Always before, *everyone* had talked about *my* drinking, pointing a superior finger and saying, "You shouldn't drink so much," "Why don't you drink like I do?" And, "You really should stop drinking."

I kept saying, "Me, too, me, too; I did that, too," as she talked about herself. I believed her when she said she actually had a life she enjoyed because of A.A. That evening, she said, "Rena, you have gone 12 hours without a drink. If you don't drink alcohol for the *next* 12 hours, you'll have 24 hours, and that's how we do it in A.A., *one day at a time. **This is a spiritual program**.* I suggest you get on your knees and ask God to help you stay away from that first drink tonight. If you have trouble doing that, throw a shoe under the bed, and while you are on your knees getting the *shoe*, ask God for help." I was honest. "*Oh, I can't do that; I don't believe in God*," I cried. There was a long pause, and she gently said, "Then you lose."

I stood at a turning point — a fork in the road. I had been yearning for this all my life, although I had no name for it. I longed for this connection, a sense of peace and belonging, a warm and fuzzy feeling that everything was all right, that I was safe, understood, and accepted. In fear of losing the only person who had *ever* understood me, I said the most profound statement I'll probably ever say, "**MAYBE I'M A LITTLE BIT SPIRITUAL.**"

In my pain and fear, I experienced just enough willingness and humility to open the door to change.

This was the beginning. I did as she suggested, feeling humiliated and embarrassed as I knelt down to ask for help from something I didn't believe in or think would work. *Oh, the arrogance of that attitude!* But curiously, when I stood up, I felt a sort of peace and slept that night without a drink of alcohol. The next morning, I called her; I was so excited. "I didn't drink last night!" She said, "***Congratulations!*** That's how we do it in A.A., *one day at a time.* You are now a card-carrying member of Alcoholics Anonymous. ***Welcome home. Welcome home.***"

A.A. Journey

And so began my journey. Without being aware of it, I was practicing the Principle of humility and its manifestations of open-mindedness, willingness, teachability, and maybe a few more.

I know you think I will give you a list of principles and line them up with the Steps — a list like the one I was given so many years ago. **I'm not going to give you that list**. I think each of us comes to our own *personal* realization of these Principles in a way that works in *our* lives. *Your* list grows and changes as *you* grow and change, just as mine does. You have your own intimate, individual AHA! moments, your spiritual awakenings.

Instead, I'm going to give you a ride through my early sobriety.

God's Schoolroom

I believe that A.A. is God's schoolroom and that I learn on more than one level: the *conscious* level of learning, where I change my **behavior** to live life on life's terms, and the all-important *unconscious* level, where my thinking and my attitude are changed **because** of the change in my actions.

In the beginning, I **thought** I was just going to meetings. However, I was really learning to have healthy relationships in a safe environment, and I was practicing *the Primary Principle of humility.*

I **thought** I was just taking care of business on a daily basis. I was really learning how to practice these principles in **all** my affairs. (Remember my experience at the bank?)

I *thought* I was just going to the Women's meeting. I was really learning the *principle of Compassion*. I learned to get out of myself and really *care* for these women, and I began to believe they cared for me, warts and all.

I *thought* I was just sponsoring women. I was really learning about the authentic me, my weaknesses and my strengths, my vulnerabilities, my control issues, and my *faulty dependencies*. I was learning the Principles of humility, love, tolerance, and genuine acceptance.

I *thought* I was just listening to "How It Works" and the Traditions read at every meeting. I was really learning the value of *repetition* in replacing old ideas with new ones. So I did a calculation:

I've been sober for over 49 years. Over the years, I've averaged four meetings a week. Doing the math, I've heard "How it Works" and the Traditions read 10,192 times. 10,192 times! Imagine what else I've heard 10,192 times!

I *thought* I was just getting married to husband #4 when I was five, and he was nine years sober. *Thank God* we had two loving sponsors and strong A.A. programs! As soon as we married and began living together, Bill and I fearfully and aggressively retreated into our old *dysfunctional* control modes and headed to the divorce court! *Thank God* we had each made a 100% commitment to our marriage. Do you know what a 99% commitment is? Dancing with the love of my life while looking over his shoulder to see if somebody better is coming along. *That was my first three marriages* and every relationship I'd ever had! *Our* Marital Recovery Program included all 12 Steps, all 12 Traditions, and *every* PRINCIPLE known to man, especially the Principles of Humility and Unity.

I *thought* I was just saying my prayers. I was really learning how to fit myself to be of maximum service to God and those about me. I was really practicing the Principles of love and tolerance.

Harmony

Living by these Principles, I am free from "the bondage of self." As St. Francis' Prayer says, I am loved and able to love. Through the miracle of A.A., I am at peace with the woman I drank to escape from — ME. The person who had to change was the person I was **before** a drink of alcohol. It's not the *drinking* person who has to change — stopping drinking does that. I'm overjoyed to be useful; I am excited to *be me*. I have learned to live in harmonious, comfortable relationships with **you**, my **God**, and **me. Just like the little girl in my story**, I am in *love* with Alcoholics Anonymous; I *love* my real life, and I *love* my real, ongoing story.

This is not the end of my story. I will continue to practice these Principles and stay close to my God through you. It has been a privilege and an honor to share my story with you. I can't *wait* to see what happens next and what God has in store *for each of us* as we trudge this Road of Happy Destiny.

Namaste.

Three Houses

DR. BOB'S HOME
855 Ardmore Ave.
Akron, Ohio 44302
(330) 864-1935

This small house on a quiet street in Akron, Ohio, was home to Dr. Bob Smith and his wife, Anne. It was here that Alcoholics Anonymous, a movement that has changed countless lives, was born in 1935, with Dr. Bob Smith and Bill Wilson as co-founders. This house holds the history of the miracle of recovery that began for Dr. Bob and hundreds of men and women around the world, making it a place of great historical significance.

Dr. Bob's home is not just a historical site, but also a 501(c)(3) non-profit organization (EIN 34-1461210) dedicated to maintaining, restoring, and preserving the property. It is through the tireless efforts of this organization that visitors, alcoholics and non-alcoholics alike, can experience the atmosphere in which our beloved fellowship was born.

THE WILSON HOUSE
P.O.Box 46
378 Village Street
East Dorset, Vermont 05253
(802) 362-5524

Owned by his grandparents, the Wilson House, a small hotel in East Dorset, Vermont, was home to Bill Wilson, co-founder of Alcoholics Anonymous. Bill W. was born there, raised there, and he and Lois are buried in the family graveyard near the Wilson House.

In 1987, the Wilson House was bought, restored, and reopened as a tribute to "Bill W." A non-profit foundation owns the property, and volunteers serve and operate the hotel. A.A. meetings and weekend retreats are held regularly at Wilson House. There is no advertising to attract guests; nevertheless, people from all over the world find their way to Bill Wilson's birthplace.

STEPPING STONES
62 Oak Rd.
Katonah, N.Y. 10536
(914) 232-4822

Stepping Stones Foundation is a privately run, tax-exempt, non-profit 501(c)(3) organization (Federal ID # 13-303-1164) that operates, preserves, and saves this National Historic Landmark home and its archives. Stepping Stones offers opportunities to explore Bill and Lois Wilson's history, legacy, and their beloved home, writing studio, and grounds where they lived and worked from 1941 until their deaths in 1971 and 1988, respectively.

The mission of the Stepping Stones Foundation is to foster public understanding of alcoholism and inspire recovery by preserving and sharing their historic home and archives. The legacy lives on through Stepping Stones, the legacy of Bill Wilson, Co-founder of Alcoholics Anonymous, and Bill's wife Lois, co-founder of the Al-Anon Family Groups.

About the Author

Rena believes her real life began the day she admitted complete defeat and joined the winning team – in other words, when she claimed powerlessness over addiction and followed a sober stranger's suggestions. With the guidance of many wise people, she turned the spotlight on herself and began her journey into the unknown.

She has spent half a century *learning* how to be "sober." Who knew it involved so much more than "just not drinking?"

Rena lives in South Florida and loves her sober life. When she is at home, Rena enjoys spending time with her husband, Cole, and her friends, both in and out of A.A.

She is passionate about Alcoholics Anonymous, the privilege of sponsorship, the joy of fellowship, and the excitement of attending conferences and sometimes sharing her experience, strength, and hope with others at conferences around the world.

You can find Rena at
https://recoveryandmore.info/